Fisher-Price®

KINDERGARTEN LEARNING PAD

Let's Read and Write

MODERN PUBLISHING
A Division of Unisystems, Inc.
New York, New York 10022

NOTE TO PARENTS

Dear Parents:

Helping your children master their world through early learning is as easy as the Fisher-Price® Learning Pads!

As your child's first and most important teacher, you can encourage your child's love of learning by participating in learning activities at home. Working together on the activities in each of the Fisher-Price® Kindergarten Learning Pads will help your child build confidence, learn to reason, and develop reading, writing, math and language skills.

Help make your time together enjoyable and rewarding by following these suggestions:

- Choose a quiet time when you and your child are relaxed.
- Provide a selection of writing materials (pens, pencils, or crayons).
- Discuss each page. Help your child relate the concepts in the books to everyday experiences.
- Only work on a few pages at a time. Don't attempt to complete every page if your child becomes tired or loses interest.
- Praise your child's efforts.

This title, Let's Read and Write, teaches the following essential skills:

√ fine motor skills and eye/hand coordination

√ forming the shapes, curves, and angles that build letters

√ reading, tracing, writing, and sounding out letters

√ following alphabetical order

√ distinguishing uppercase and lowercase letters

√ reading, writing, and understanding basic vocabulary words

√ reading, writing, and understanding numbers.

Collect the entire series of Fisher-Price® Kindergarten Learning Pads:

- Let's Try Math
- Let's Try Phonics
- Let's Read and Write
- Let's Think

Choo! Choo! Here comes the railroad train!
Can you find four things that don't belong in this picture?
Circle the four things.

Skills: Recognizing differences; Noticing details

Ahoy, mates!
Help the pirates get back to their ship.
Draw a line through the maze.

Finish

Start

Skills: Developing fine motor skills

Let's visit the park!
Look closely at both pictures.
Find four things in the top picture that are
missing from the bottom picture.
Circle the four things.

Skills: Recognizing differences; Noticing details

Look at each picture.
Find the circles.
Put a **ring** around them.
Find the squares.
Put an **X** on them.

circle

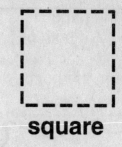

square

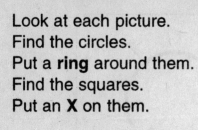

Skills: Recognizing shapes; Building vocabulary

A Perfect Picnic

Look at this picture.
Find the triangles.
Color them.
Find the rectangles.
Put an **X** on them.
Find the diamonds.
Put a **ring** around them.

 **triangle**
 **diamond**
 **rectangle**

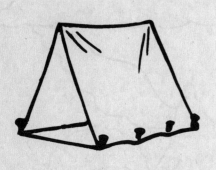

Skills: Recognizing shapes; Building vocabulary

What's wrong with this picture?
Find four things that don't belong at the beach.
Put an **X** on each one.

Skills: Logical reasoning; Noticing details

Can you write the alphabet?
Trace each letter.
Say each letter name.

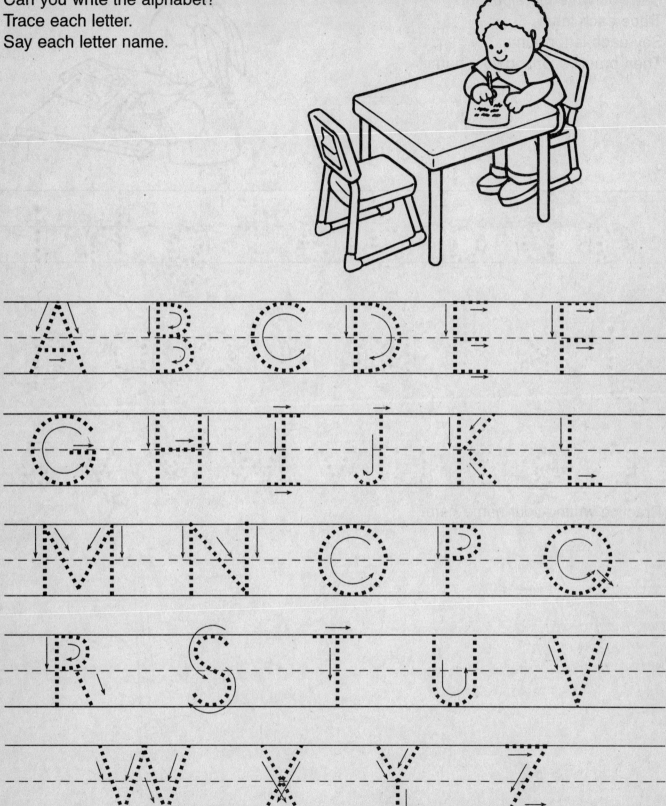

A B C D E F
G H I J K L
M N O P Q
R S T U V
W X Y Z

Skills: Letter order; Forming uppercase letters; Writing the alphabet; Saying letter names

Can you write the alphabet?
Trace each letter.
Say each letter name.
Then practice writing your name.

a b c d e f g h i

j k l m n o p q

r s t u v w x y z

Practice writing your name here.

Skills: Letter order; Forming lowercase letters; Writing the alphabet; Saying letter names

Who's hiding in the grass?
To find out, connect the dots from **A** to **Z**.
Then color the picture.

Skills: Letter order; Recognizing uppercase letters

All aboard!
Look at the letters in each train.
What letter comes next?
Write the missing letter.

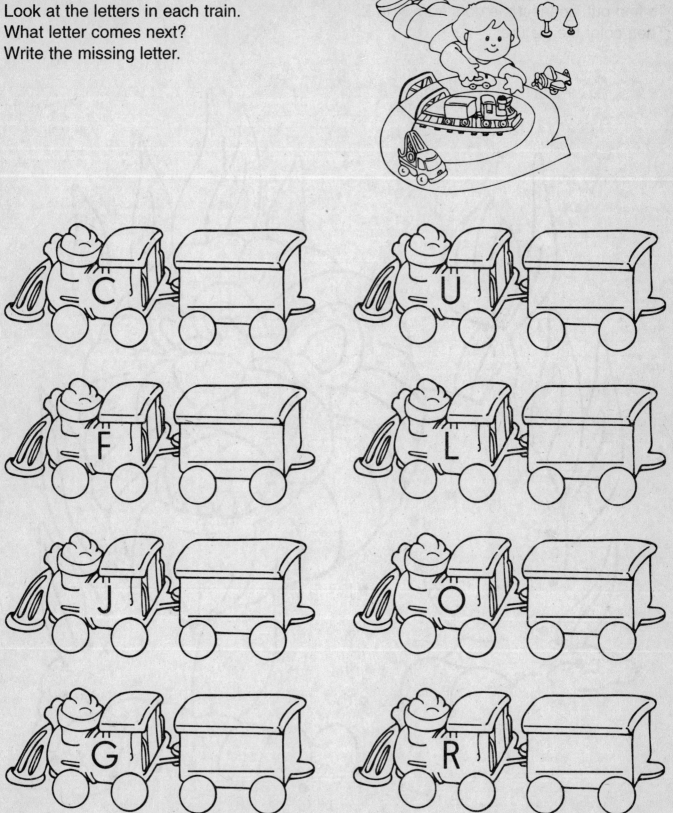

C

U

F

L

J

O

G

R

Skills: Letter order; Recognizing uppercase letters

Let's go for a ride!
Look at the letter on each helmet.
What letter comes before?
Write the missing letter.

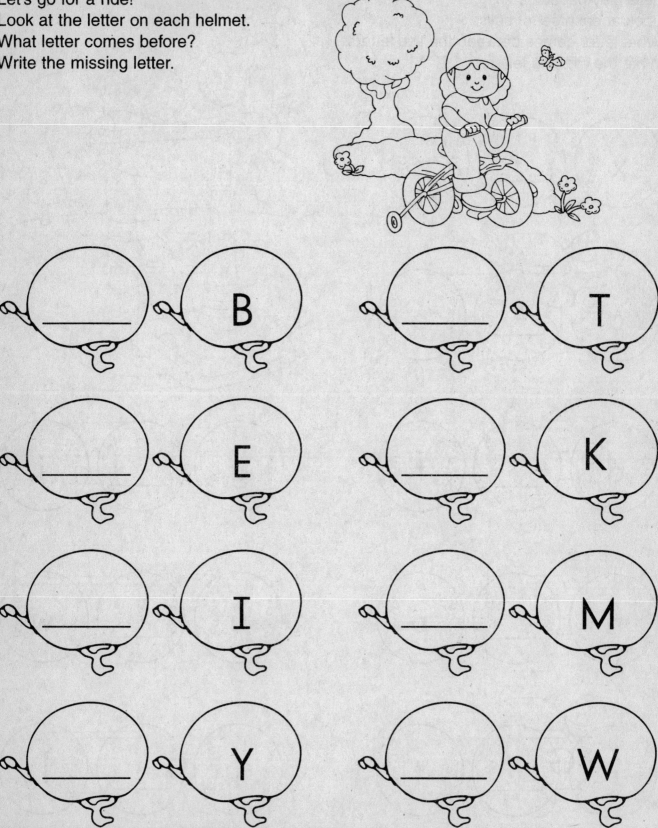

_____ B   _____ T

_____ E   _____ K

_____ I   _____ M

_____ Y   _____ W

Skills: Letter order; Recognizing uppercase letters

Let's play baseball!
Look at each set of balls.
What letter comes between the two letters?
Write the missing letter.

x __ z

a __ c

d __ f   g __ i

n __ p   u __ w

r __ t   j __ l

Skills: Letter order; Recognizing lowercase letters

Time to cool off!
Use the code to color the picture.

Color each **A** space white.
Color each **B** space red.
Color each **C** space blue.
Color each **D** space yellow.
Color each **E** space orange.
Color each **F** space black.

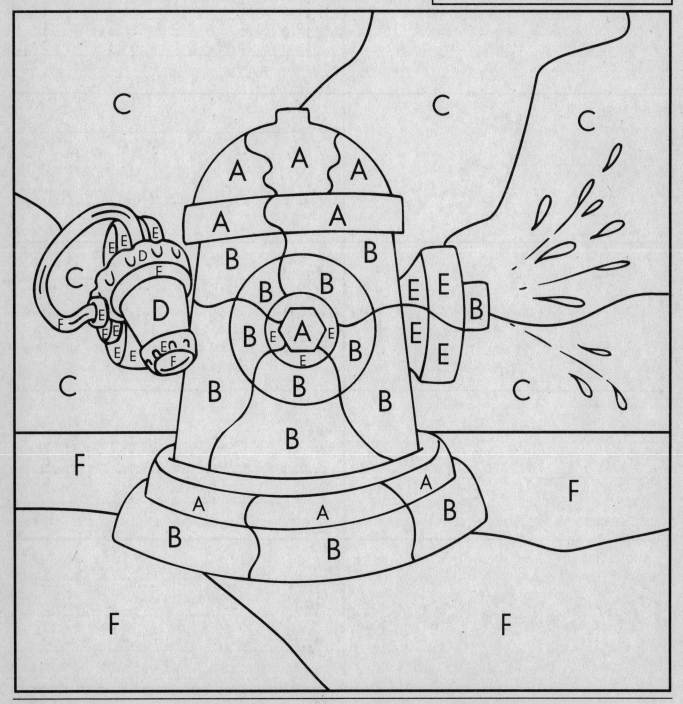

Skills: Distinguishing color; Matching shapes to color codes; Building vocabulary

Let's get set to count!
Count the items in each row.
Then trace the numbers.

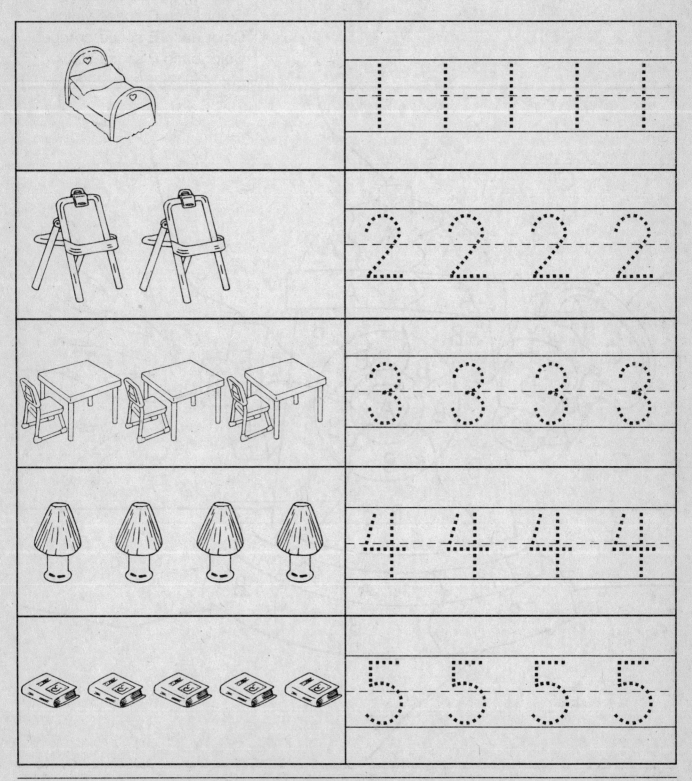

Skills: Recognizing and writing numbers; Counting

Count higher and higher!
Count the things in each row.
Then trace the numbers.

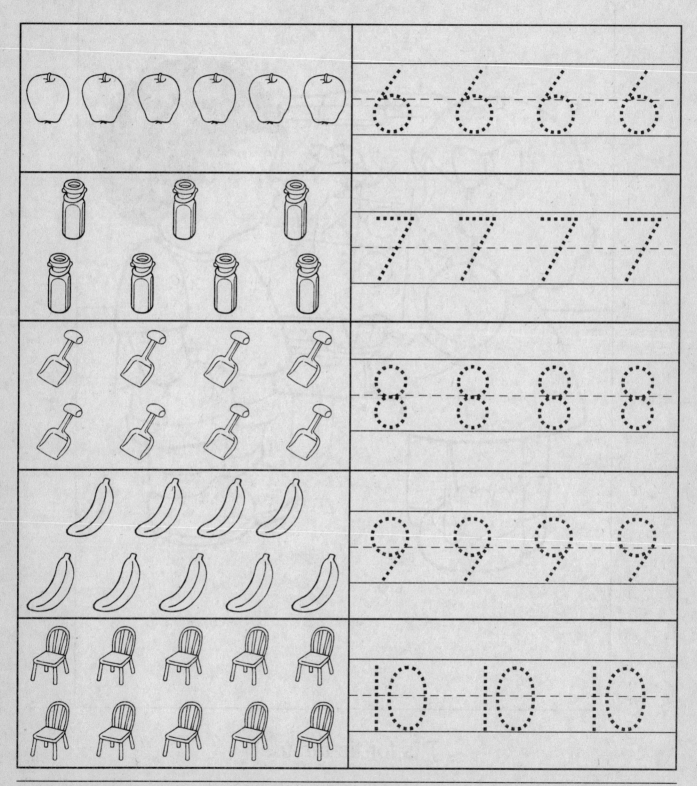

Skills: Recognizing and writing numbers; Counting

T is for tic-tac-toe!

What did the children build?
To find out, connect the dots from **1** to **15**.
Then color the picture.

Skills: Number order; Recognizing numbers 1-15

It's fun to dress up!
What will you be?
Use the code to color
the picture and find out.

Color each **1** space red.
Color each **2** space yellow.
Color each **3** space blue.
Color each **4** space green.
Color each **5** space purple.

Skills: Distinguishing color; Matching shapes to color codes; Building vocabulary

Let's go fishing!
Look at each group of fish.
What number comes next?
Write the number that comes next.

Let's play dress-up!
Look at each group of hats.
What number comes before?
Write the missing number.

___ 5

___ 2

___ 7

___ 4

___ 3

___ 9

___ 8

___ 6

Skills: Number order; Recognizing numbers

Look at each set of Baby's First Blocks.
What number comes in between?
Write the number.

Skills: Number order; Recognizing numbers

Ring! Ring! Let's make a telephone call.
Write your name and telephone number.

Skills: Writing name and telephone number

Special delivery!
The mail carrier has a letter for you.
What does the envelope say?
Write your name and address.

Skills: Writing name and address

Color the crayon to match the word.
Trace the word.
Then write the color word under each picture.
Color the rest of the page.

red

yellow

red

yellow

Skills: Identifying color words; Building and writing vocabulary

Color the crayon to match the word.
Trace the word.
Then write the color word under each picture.
Color the rest of the page.

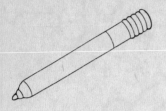 green

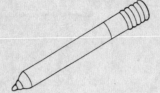 blue

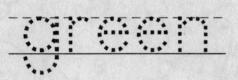

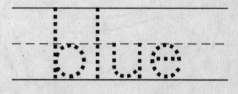

_____

- - - - - - - - - -

_____

_____

- - - - - - - - - -

_____

_____

- - - - - - - - - -

_____

_____

- - - - - - - - - -

_____

Skills: Identifying color words; Building and writing vocabulary

Building Buddies

Let's paint a picture.
What colors will you use?
Read the color words.
Then color the paints to match!

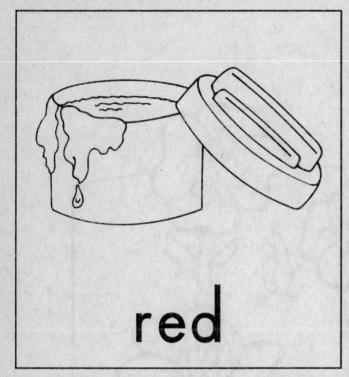

red

yellow

green

blue

Skills: Recognizing color names; Building vocabulary

Spring is blooming!
What animal might you see in the garden?
Draw it! Then color the picture.
Then trace and write the word.

spring

Skills: Developing fine motor skills; Eye/hand coordination; Building and writing vocabulary

There's lots to do in the summer.
What might be flying in the sky above?
Draw it! Then color the picture.
Then trace and write the word.

summer

Skills: Developing fine motor skills; Eye/hand coordination; Building and writing vocabulary

The leaves fall down in fall!
Trees come in all shapes and sizes.
Draw some here. Then color the picture.
Then trace and write the word.

f a l l

Skills: Developing fine motor skills; Eye/hand coordination; Building and writing vocabulary

Winter is the time to bundle up!
There's a lot you can do on a snowy hill.
Draw one here! Then color the picture.
Then trace and write the word.

winter

Skills: Developing fine motor skills; Eye/hand coordination; Building and writing vocabulary

The horse is **first**.

Look at the pictures in each row.
Circle the **first** picture in each row.
Then trace and write the word.

first ┆first┆

Skills: Recognizing ordinal numbers (first); Position; Building and writing vocabulary

The cow is **second**.

Look at the pictures in each row.
Circle the **second** picture in each row.
Then trace and write the word.

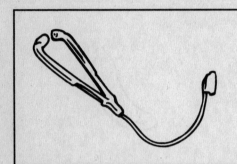  

second

Skills: Recognizing ordinal numbers (second); Position; Building and writing vocabulary

The hen is **third**.

Look at the pictures in each row.
Circle the **third** picture in each row.
Then trace and write the word.

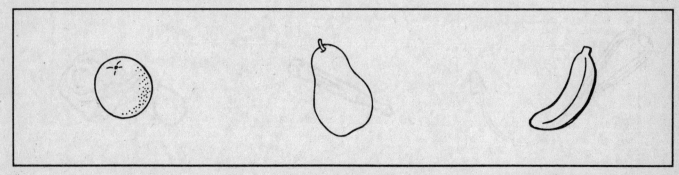

third
        t h i r d

Skills: Recognizing ordinal numbers (third); Position; Building and writing vocabulary

"Feeding fish is fun!"

The star is **in**.
The triangle is **out**.

Look at the picture in each box.
Circle the one that is **in**.
Put an **X** on the one that is **out**.
Then trace and write the words **in** and **out**.

Skills: Recognizing location (in and out); Building and writing vocabulary

The helicopter is **over** the tree.
The truck is **under** the tree.

Look at the picture in each box.
Circle the one that is **over**.
Put an **X** on the one that is **under**.
Then trace the words **over** and **under**.

over

under

Skills: Recognizing location (over); Building and writing vocabulary

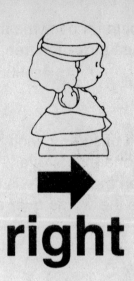

left

right

Look at the people on this page.
Are they facing **left** or **right**?
Write a word under each picture to
tell which way the people are facing.

_____

- - - - - - - - - - - - - - - -

_____

_____

- - - - - - - - - - - - - - - -

_____

Skills: Recognizing right and left; Building and writing vocabulary

The words up and down, on and off, same and different are opposites.
Look at each picture.
Trace the word that describes it.

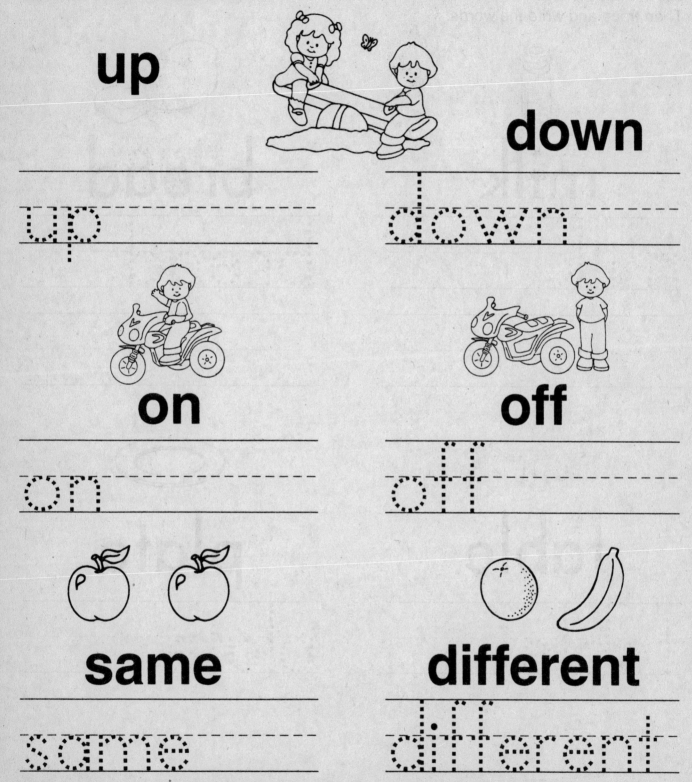

up

down

up

down

on

off

on

off

same

different

same

different

Skills: Recognizing opposites (up, down); Building and writing vocabulary

Let's go into the kitchen.
What do we see?
Look at the pictures and read the words.
Then trace and write the words.

milk

milk

bread

bread

table

table

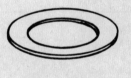

plate

plate

Skills: Categorizing; Building and writing vocabulary

ANSWER KEY

Page 4

Choo! Choo! Here comes the railroad train!
Can you find four things that don't belong in this picture?
Circle the four things.

Page 5

Ahoy, mates!
Help the pirates get back to their ship.
Draw a line through the maze.

Page 6

Let's visit the park!
Look closely at both pictures.
Find four things in the top picture that are
missing from the bottom picture.
Circle the four things.

Page 7

Look at each picture.
Find the circles.
Put a ring around them.
Find the squares.
Put an X on them.

circle   square

Skills: Recognizing shapes; Building vocabulary

Page 9

Look at this picture.
Find the triangles.
Color them.
Find the rectangles.
Put an X on them.
Find the diamonds.
Put a ring around them.

triangle   diamond   rectangle

Skills: Recognizing shapes; Building vocabulary

Page 10

What's wrong with this picture?
Find four things that don't belong at the beach.
Put an X on each one.

Page 13

Who's hiding in the grass?
To find out, connect the dots from **A** to **Z**.
Then color the picture.

Page 14

All aboard!
Look at the letters in each train.
What letter comes next?
Write the missing letter.

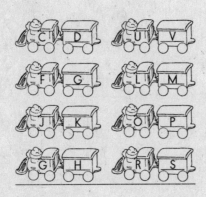

Page 15

Let's go for a ride!
Look at the letter on each helmet.
What letter comes before?
Write the missing letter.

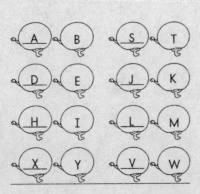

Page 16

Let's play baseball!
Look at each set of balls.
What letter comes between the two letters?
Write the missing letter.

Skills: Letter order; Recognizing lowercase letters

Page 21

What did the children build?
To find out, connect the dots from 1 to **15**.
Then color the picture.

Page 23

Let's go fishing!
Look at each group of fish.
What number comes next?
Write the number that comes next.

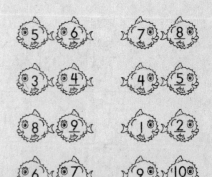

ANSWER KEY

Page 24

Let's play dress-up!
Look at each group of hats.
What number comes before?
Write the missing number.

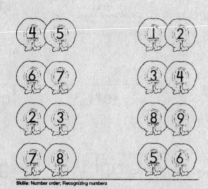

Skills: Number order; Recognizing numbers

Page 25

Look at each set of Baby's First Blocks.
What number comes in between?
Write the number.

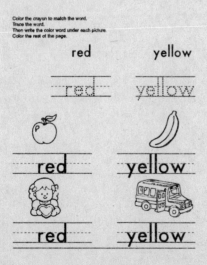

Page 28

Color the crayon to match the word.
Trace the word.
Then write the color word under each picture.
Color the rest of the page.

red   yellow

red   yellow

red   yellow

Page 29

Color the crayon to match the word.
Trace the word.
Then write the color word under each picture.
Color the rest of the page.

green   blue

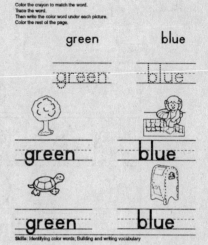

green   blue

green   blue

Skills: Identifying color words; Building and writing vocabulary

Page 36

The horse is **first**.

Look at the pictures in each row.
Circle the **first** picture in each row.
Then trace and write the word.

first   first   first

Skills: Recognizing ordinal numbers (first); Position; Building and writing vocabulary

Page 37

The cow is **second**.

Look at the pictures in each row.
Circle the **second** picture in each row.
Then trace and write the word.

second   second   second

Skills: Recognizing ordinal numbers (second); Position; Building and writing vocabulary

ANSWER KEY

Page 38

The hen is **third**.

Look at the pictures in each row.
Circle the third picture in each row.
Then trace and write the word.

third ~~third~~ **third**

Skills: Recognizing ordinal numbers (third); Position; Building and writing vocabulary

Page 40

The star is **in**.
The triangle is **out**.

Look at the picture in each box.
Circle the one that is **in**.
Put an X on the one that is **out**.
Then trace and write the words **in** and **out**.

~~in~~ in ~~out~~ out

Skills: Recognizing location (in and out); Building and writing vocabulary

Page 41

The helicopter is **over** the tree.
The truck is **under** the tree.

Look at the picture in each box.
Circle the one that is **over**.
Put an X on the one that is **under**.
Then trace the words **over** and **under**.

~~over~~ ~~under~~

Page 42

← **left** → **right**

Look at the people on this page.
Are they facing **left** or **right**?
Write a word under each picture to
tell which way the people are facing.

left   left

right   right